Hal•Leonard®
Piano Play-Along

PIANO | VOCAL | GUITAR • AUDIO

VOLUME 126

BRUNO MARS

AUDIO
ACCESS
INCLUDED

PLAYBACK+
Speed • Pitch • Balance • Loop

To access audio visit:
www.halleonard.com/mylibrary

Enter Code
5764-4966-7564-1166

Cover photo: Kevin Kane/FilmMagic/Getty Images

ISBN 978-1-4803-6061-7

HAL•LEONARD®

7777 W. BLUEMOUND RD. P.O. BOX 13819 MILWAUKEE, WI 53213

In Australia Contact:
Hal Leonard Australia Pty. Ltd.
4 Lentara Court
Cheltenham, Victoria, 3192 Australia
Email: ausadmin@halleonard.com.au

Visit Hal Leonard Online at
www.halleonard.com

COUNT ON ME

Words and Music by BRUNO MARS,
ARI LEVINE and PHILIP LAWRENCE

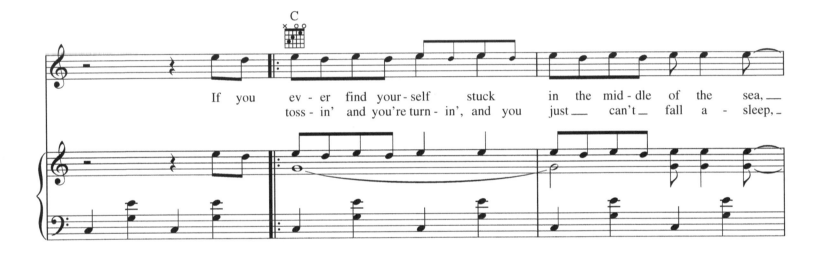

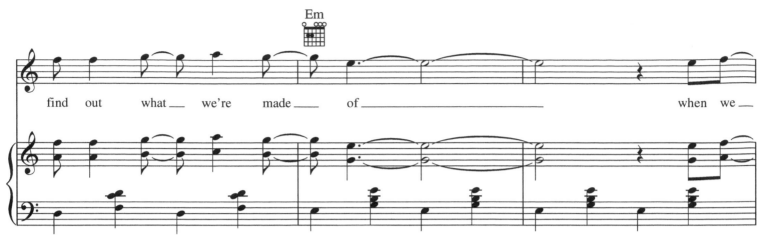

find out what __ we're made __ of _____ when we __

__ are called __ to help _____ our friends _ in need. ____

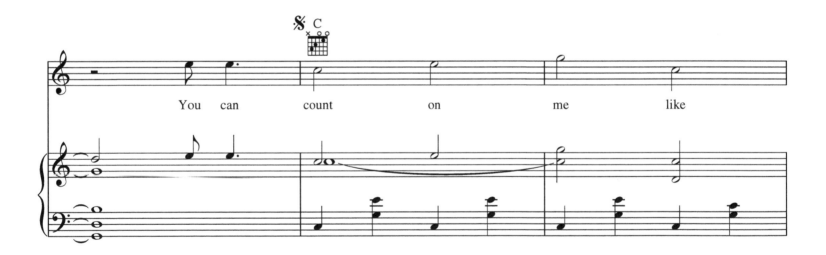

You can count on me like

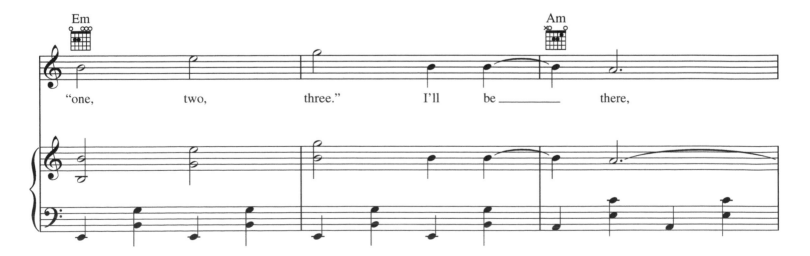

"one, two, three." I'll be _____ there,

and I know when I need it. I can

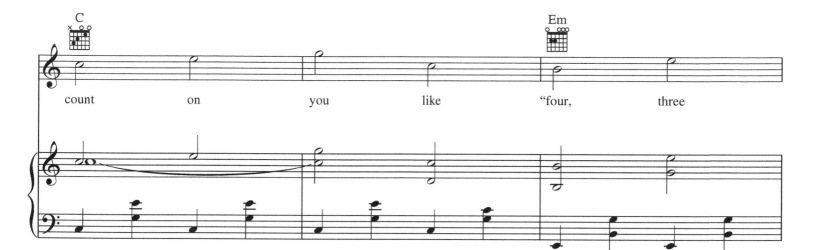

count on you like "four, three

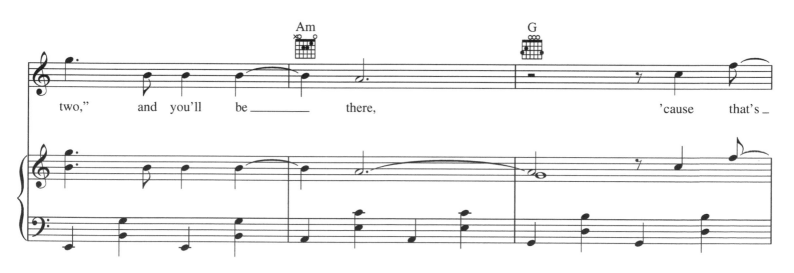

two," and you'll be _____ there, 'cause that's _

_ what friends _ are s'posed _ to do, ___ oh, yeah. ___ Ooh, _

To Coda ⊕

ooh,

yeah, yeah. If you're

yeah. You'll al - ways have my
nev - er have let go,

shoul - der when you cry.
nev - er say good -

GRENADE

Words and Music by BRUNO MARS,
ARI LEVINE, PHILIP LAWRENCE,
BRODY BROWN, CLAUDE KELLY
and ANDREW WYATT

Easy come, easy go; that's just how you live. Oh,

take, take, take it all, but you nev-er give.

Should-'ve known you was trou-ble from the first kiss; had your

bul - let straight through my brain. _____ Yes, I would die ____

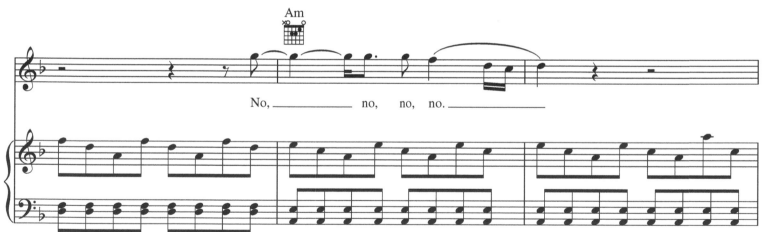

To Coda ⊕

____ for you, ba - by, but you won't do the same.

No, _____ no, no, no. _____

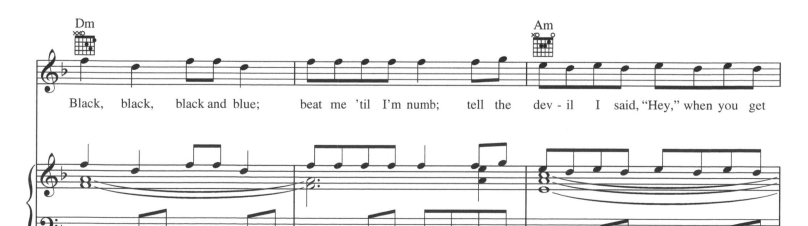

Black, black, black and blue; beat me 'til I'm numb; tell the dev - il I said, "Hey," when you get

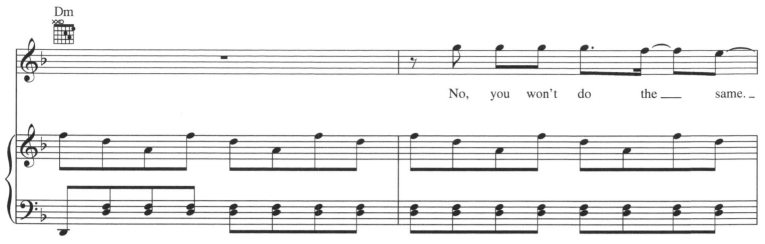

No, you won't do the ___ same. ___

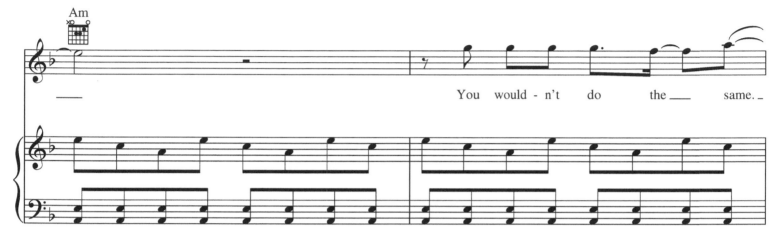

___ You would-n't do the ___ same. ___

_____ Ooh, ___ you nev - er do the ___ same, ___

___ no, _____ no, no, no. _____

IT WILL RAIN
from the Summit Entertainment film THE TWILIGHT SAGA: BREAKING DAWN – PART 1

Words and Music by BRUNO MARS,
PHILIP LAWRENCE and ARI LEVINE

Moderate groove

If you ev-er leave me, ba-by,

leave some mor-phine at my door.

'Cause it would take a whole lot of med-i-ca-tion

to re - a - lize what we used to have, _ we don't have it an - y - more. _____

There's no re - li - gion that __ could save __ me,

no mat - ter how long my __ knees are on the floor. __ Oh. _____

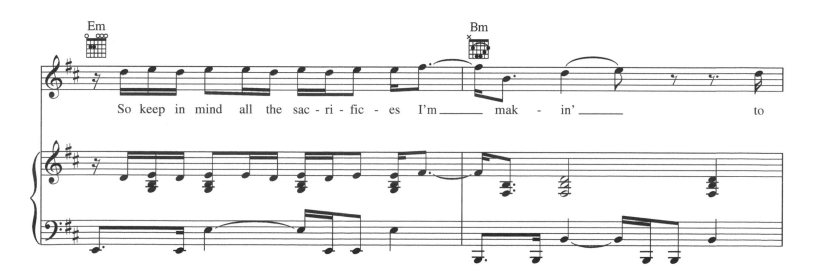

So keep in mind all the sac - ri - fic - es I'm ____ mak - in' ____ to

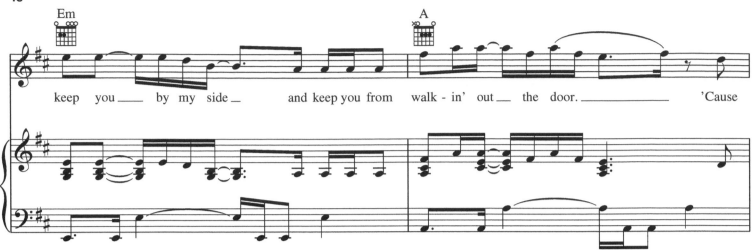

keep you ___ by my side ___ and keep you from walk - in' out ___ the door. _____ 'Cause

there'll be no sun - light if I lose you, ba - by.

There'll be no clear ___ skies if I lose you, ba - by.

Just like the clouds, my eyes ___ will do the same. ___ If you ___ walk a-

way, _____ ev - 'ry day it - 'll rain, ____ rain, ____ rain. ___

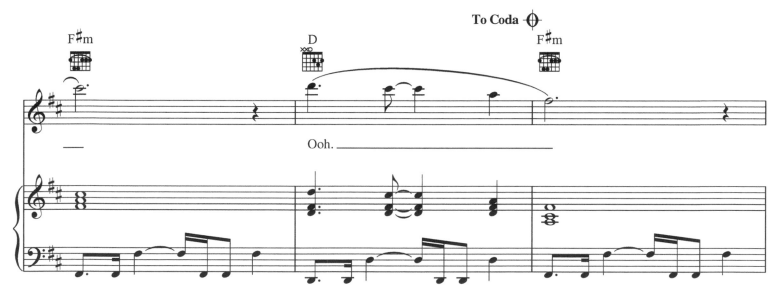

Ooh. _____

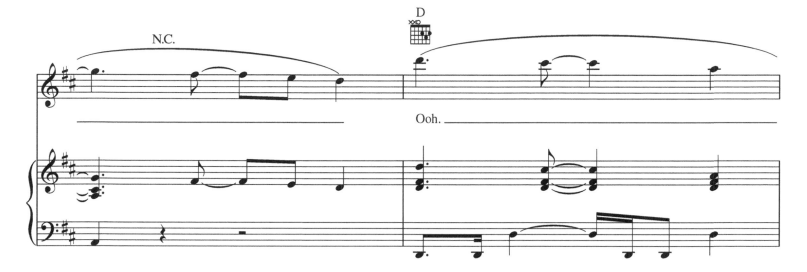

Ooh. _____

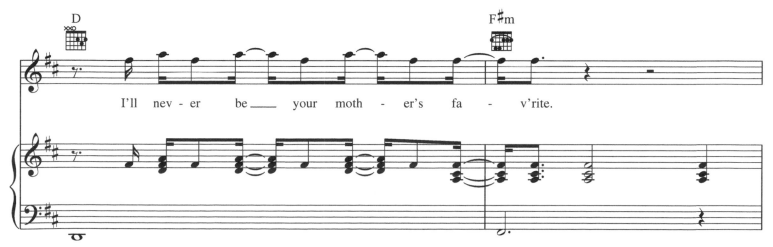

I'll nev - er be ____ your moth - er's fa - v'rite.

Your dad - dy can't e - ven look _ me in _ the eye. _ Ooh. ____

If I was in their shoes, _ I'd be do - in' the ___ same _ thing, ____ say - ing

there goes _ my lit - tle girl _ walk - ing with that _ trou - ble - some _ guy. _____ But they're _

_ just a - fraid _ of some - thing they _ can't un - der - stand. Ooh. ____

But, lit-tle dar-ling, watch _ me change _ their minds. Yeah, for you I'll try, _

_ I'll try, _ I'll try, _ I'll try _____ and pick up these bro-

D.S. al Coda

- ken piec-es 'til _ I'm bleed-in' if that -'ll make _ you mine. _____ 'Cause

CODA

Oh, _ don't just say _____ good - bye. _

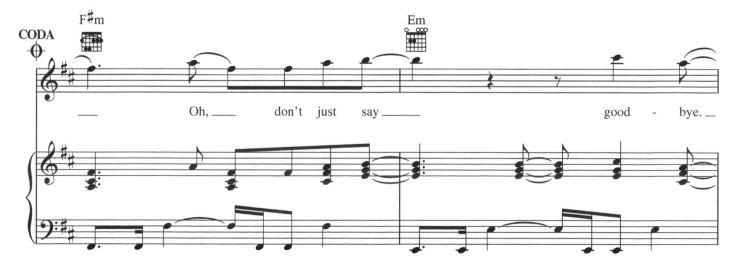

if I lose you, ba - by. And just like the clouds, — my eyes —

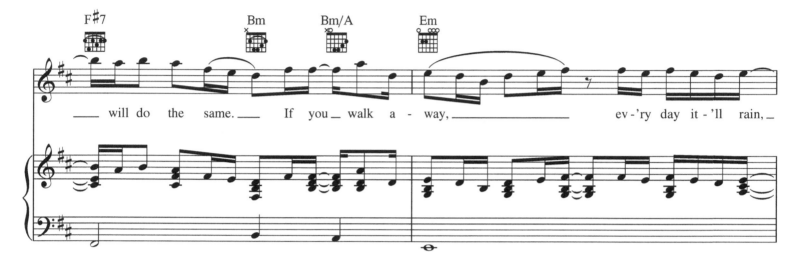

— will do the same. — If you — walk a - way, _____ ev -'ry day it -'ll rain, —

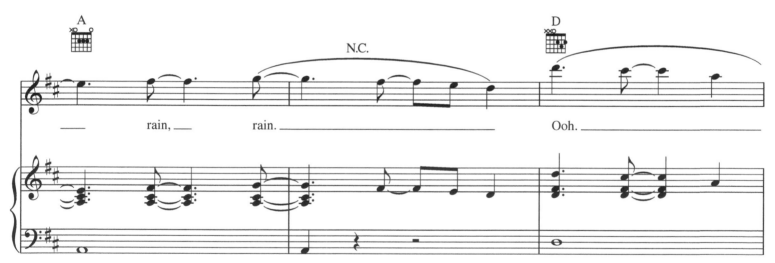

— rain, — rain. _____ Ooh. _____

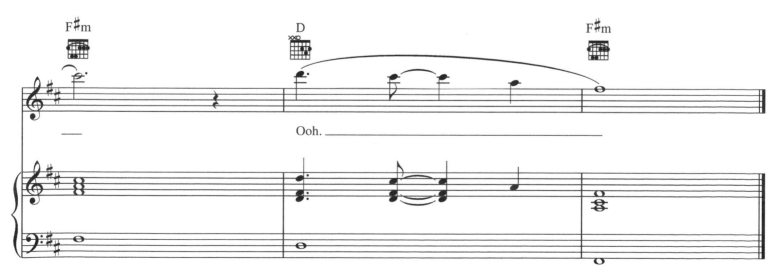

— Ooh. _____

JUST THE WAY YOU ARE

Words and Music by BRUNO MARS,
ARI LEVINE, PHILIP LAWRENCE,
KHARI CAIN and KHALIL WALTON

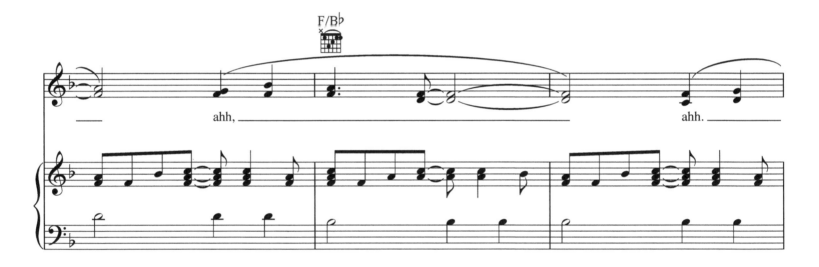

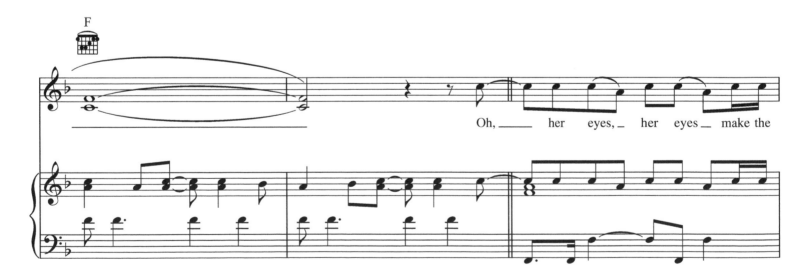

stars look like they're not shin - in'. Her hair, her hair falls per - fect - ly with - out her try - in'.

She's so beau - ti - ful, and I tell her ev - 'ry day.

Yeah. I know, I know when I com - pli - ment her, she won't be - lieve me.

And it's so, it's so sad to think that she don't see what I see.

But ev-'ry time _ she asks _ me, "Do _ I look _ o - kay?" _ I _ say: _

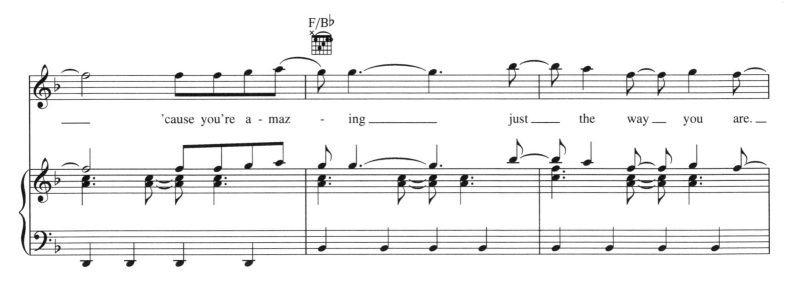

When I see your face, _ there's not a thing _ that I _ would change, _

_ 'cause you're a - maz - ing _ just _ the way _ you are. _

_ And when you smile, _

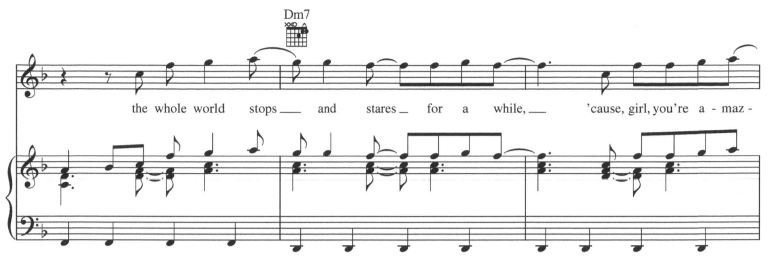

the whole world stops __ and stares __ for a while, __ 'cause, girl, you're a - maz -

- ing _____ just __ the way __ you are. __

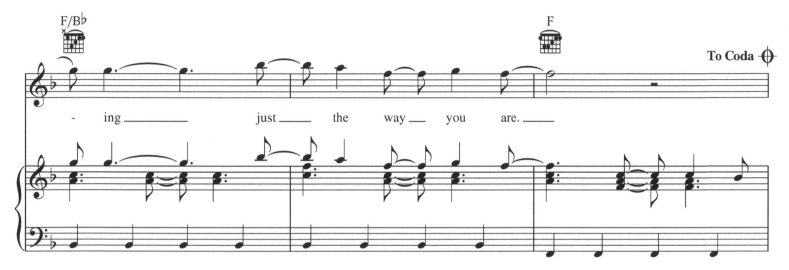

Yeah. __ Her lips, __ her lips, __ I could kiss them all __ day if __ she'd let me.

Her laugh, _ her laugh, _ she hates but I __ think it's __ so sex - y. She's so beau - ti - ful, __

and I tell her ev - 'ry_____ day.   Oh,   you

know, you know, you know I'd nev - er ask you to change. _   If per-fect's what you're search-in' for then

just stay   the same. _   So _____   don't e - ven both - er ask - in' if _

D.S. al Coda

_ you look_ o - kay. _   You know I'll   say: _____   When I see your   face, _

CODA

The way ___ you are, ___   the way ___ you are. ___

Dm7   F/Bb

Girl, you're a - maz - ing ___ just ___

F

___ the way ___ you are. ___   When I see your face, ___

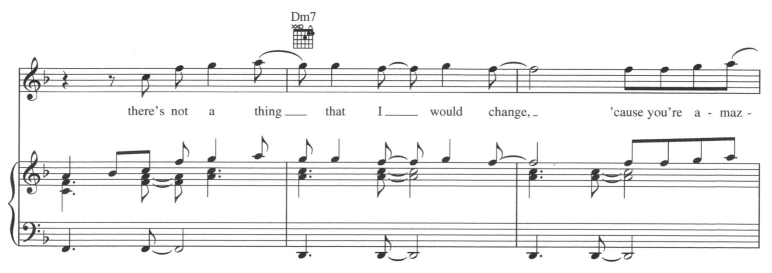

Dm7

there's not a thing ___ that I ___ would change, ___ 'cause you're a - maz -

-ing just the way you are.

And when you smile, the whole world stops

and stares for a while, 'cause, girl, you're a-maz-ing just

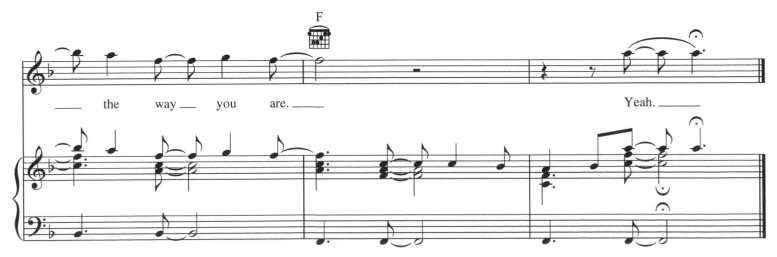

the way you are. Yeah.

MARRY YOU

Words and Music by BRUNO MARS,
ARI LEVINE and PHILIP LAWRENCE

Moderately fast

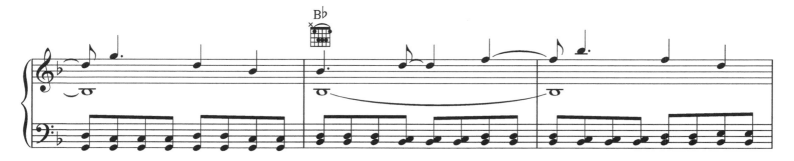

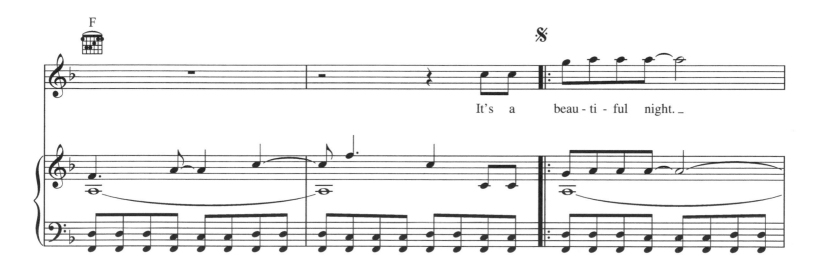

It's a beau-ti-ful night. _

We're look-ing for some-thing dumb to do. ____

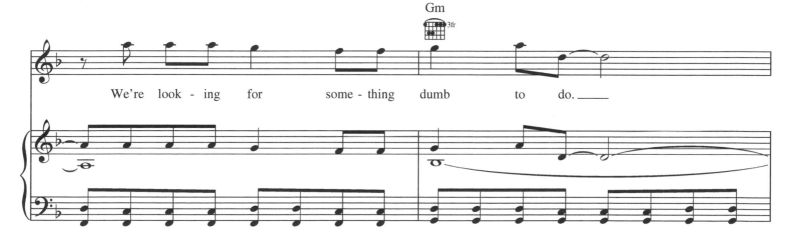

Hey, ba - by, I think I wan - na mar - ry you.

Is it the look in your eyes,

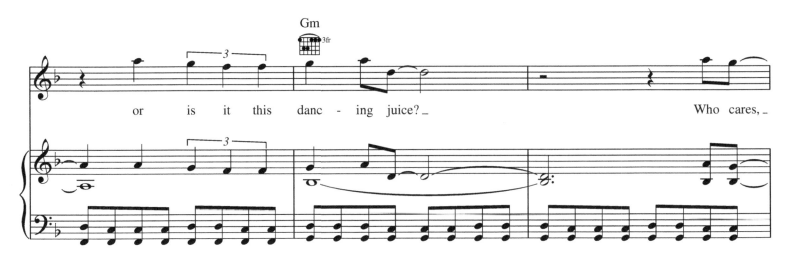

or is it this danc - ing juice? Who cares,

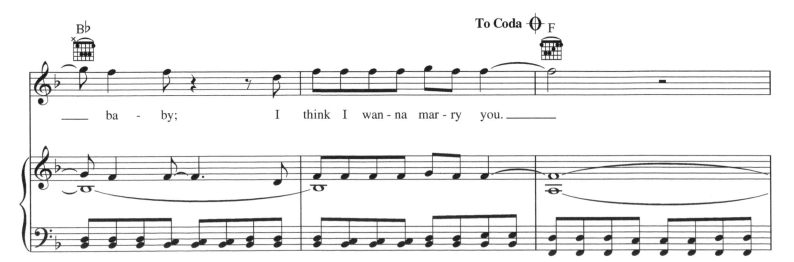

To Coda

ba - by; I think I wan - na mar - ry you.

Well, I know this lit-tle chap-el on the boul-e-vard, we can
I'll go get a ring; let the choir bells sing, like,

go. "Ooh."
No one will know.
So, what you wan-na do?

Oh, come on, girl. Who
Let's just run, girl.

cares if we're trashed, got a pock-et full of cash we can
If we wake up and you wan-na break up, that's

if you're read - y like I'm read -

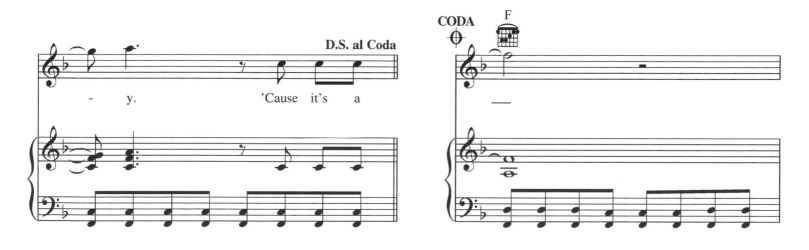

- y. 'Cause it's a - y like I'm read -

- y. 'Cause it's a

D.S. al Coda   **CODA**

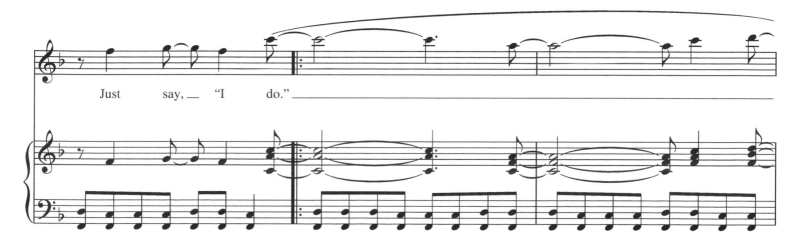

Just say, "I do."

Gm   Bb

Tell __ me right now, ba - by.

F

Tell __ me right now, ba - by. Ba - by, just say, __ "I do." __

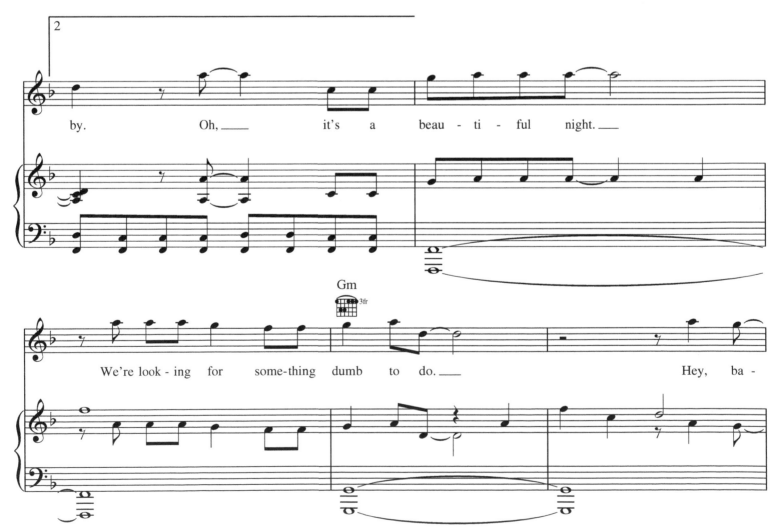

2

by. Oh, ____ it's a beau - ti - ful night. ___

Gm

We're look - ing for some - thing dumb to do. __ Hey, ba -

LOCKED OUT OF HEAVEN

Words and Music by BRUNO MARS,
ARI LEVINE and PHILIP LAWRENCE

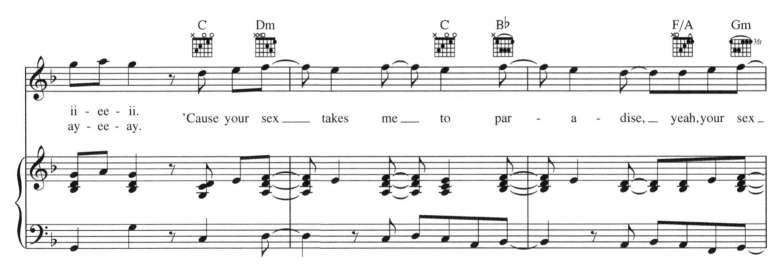

I'm born a - gain ev - 'ry time ___ you spend ___ the night, _____ ee -
And right ___ there is ___ where ___ I want ___ to stay, _____ ee -

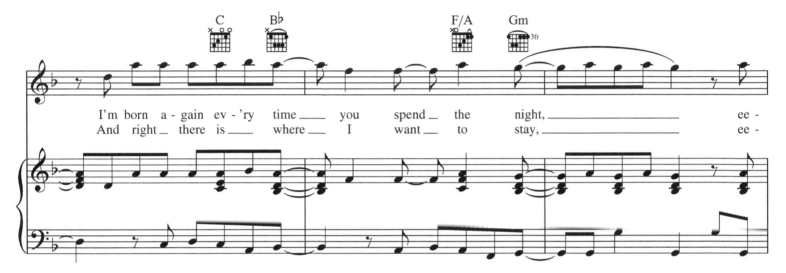

ii - ee - ii. 'Cause your sex ___ takes me ___ to par - a - dise, ___ yeah, your sex ___
ay - ee - ay.

___ takes me ___ to par - a - dise. ___ And it shows, _____

yeah, ___ yeah, ___ yeah. ___ 'Cause you make me

feel ___ like ___ I've been locked out of heav - en ___

for too long, _____ for too

long. _____ Yeah, you ___ make me feel ___ like ___

42

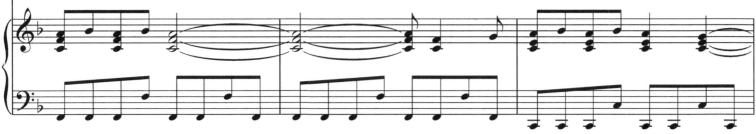

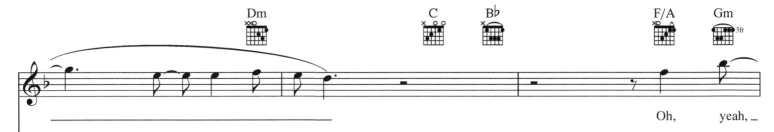

D.S. al Coda

yeah, oh, yeah, yeah, yeah, yeah.

CODA

Oh,

yeah.

Can I just stay here,

spend the rest of my days here?

'Cause you make me feel ___ like ___ I've been locked out of heav-

-en ___ for too long, _____ for too

long. _____ Yeah, you make me feel ___ like ___

I've been locked out of heav - en ___ for too

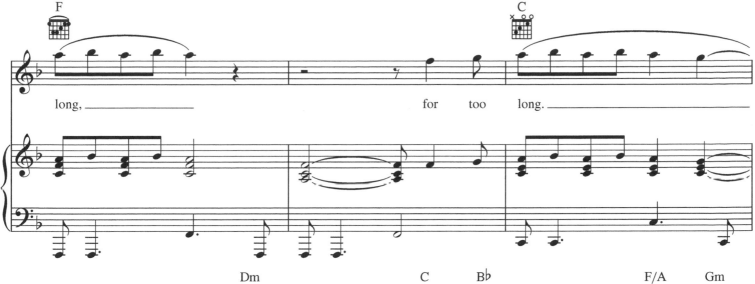

long, _____ for too long. _____

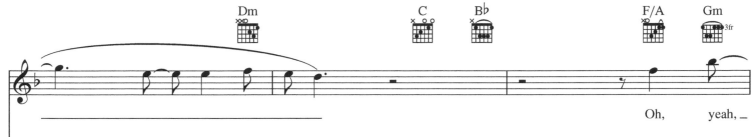

Oh, yeah, _

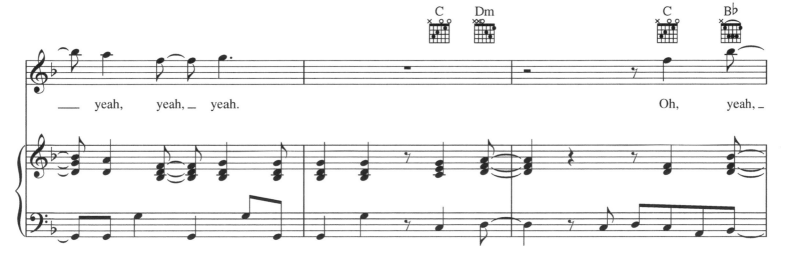

_ yeah, yeah, _ yeah. Oh, yeah, _

_ yeah, oh, yeah, _ yeah, yeah, _ yeah.

TREASURE

Words and Music by BRUNO MARS,
ARI LEVINE, PHILIP LAWRENCE
and PHREDLEY BROWN

You are my treas - ure, you are my treas - ure, you are my treas - ure, yeah,

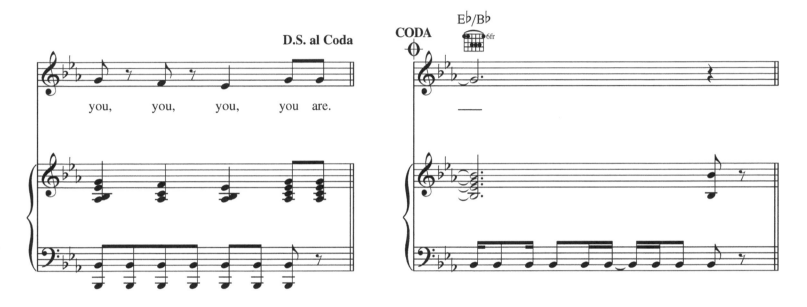

D.S. al Coda

you, you, you, you are.

CODA

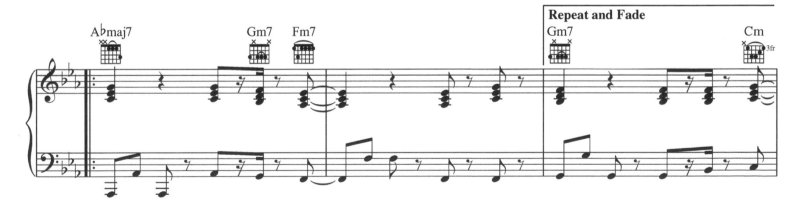

Repeat and Fade

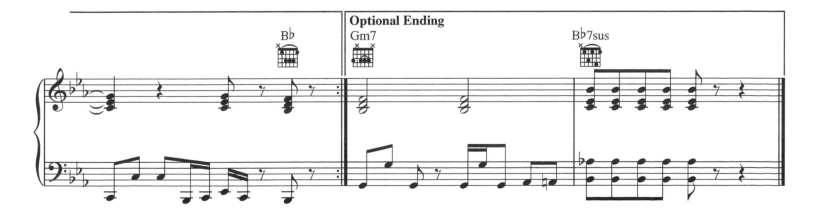

Optional Ending

WHEN I WAS YOUR MAN

Words and Music by BRUNO MARS,
ARI LEVINE, PHILIP LAWRENCE
and ANDREW WYATT